I0626413

"Color Me," Kalamazoo
Invasion of the Monster Trucks

THIS BOOK BELONGS TO _____

FIRST EDITION

Story by Darryl Breland, aka Papa D

based on the original YouTube series by Darryl Breland

Illustrated using AI-generated animation stills

Kalamazoo designed and illustrated by Anna Breland

Published by Breland Publishing

ISBN-13:
979-8-9998699-2-0

Activity Page

<< Maze / Word Search / Connecct the Dots >>

GOAL

Kalamazoo

✏️ ***Kalamazoo*** is a young boy with dark, tousled hair and large brown eyes. He wears a bright **red headband** tied around his head, with one end hanging to the side. His shirt is a **light beige short-sleeve tunic** with the sleeves rolled up, and over it he wears a **brown vest**. Around his waist is a **tan cloth belt** with a **blue sash**, tied loosely at the side. He wears **green pants** tucked into his **brown boots**. In his hand he carries a simple **wooden toy sword**.

✏️ **Color William.**

William is a young toddler boy with thick, **brown, tousled hair** and big **brown eyes**. His cheeks have dimples when he smiles. He wears a **light cream, short-sleeved shirt** with a soft collar and **three small brown buttons**. His sleeves are rolled up. He also wears **green shorts** with a simple hem and **brown shoes**.

✏️ **Color Jordan**

Jordan has bright red hair with a tousled style and light freckles on his cheeks. His eyes are **blue** and full of energy. He wears a **short-sleeve green tunic** with a small lace-up neckline, held at the waist with a **brown belt**. He also wears **brown pants** and **brown boots**.

✏️ **Color Queen Ashley**

Queen Ashley is a beautiful queen with long, flowing **red hair** and bright **blue eyes**. She wears a beautiful **deep red gown** decorated with **gold trim and patterns**. Over her head is a soft **golden veil** that flows down behind her shoulders. On her head she wears a shining **gold crown** decorated with **red and blue jewels**. She also wears **gold earrings** and a simple **gold necklace**.

✏️ **Color King Bailey**

King Bailey is a strong, brave, and mighty king, with short **brown hair**, a neatly trimmed **brown beard**, and warm **brown eyes**. He wears a regal **royal blue tunic** with **gold trim** and a **gold emblem** on the chest. Around his waist is a wide **brown belt** with a **gold buckle**. Over his shoulders he wears a flowing **red cape** with a **white fur collar**. On his head rests a shining **gold crown** with rounded tips. He also wears **royal blue pants** and tall **brown boots**.

✏️ **Color Princess Anna**

Princess Anna is a beautiful princess from the land in the east. She has long **brown hair** and bright **green eyes**. She wears a beautiful **teal gown** with flowing sleeves, decorated with **gold trim and patterns**. Around her waist is a **gold belt** that matches the gold accents on her dress. On her head she wears a delicate **gold crown** with small jewels. She also wears **gold earrings** to complete her royal look.

✏️ **Color Papa D**

Papa D has **brown hair with blond highlights** that some people mistake as being gray hair and a neatly trimmed **mix of blond and brown beard and mustache**. He wears round glasses with thin gold rims, and he has warm **hazel eyes**. His usual outfit is a **blue flannel pajama shirt** with a large-check plaid pattern and buttons down the front and matching **blue flannel pajama pants**. His footwear is soft **navy-blue slippers**.

✏️ **Color Uncle Nathan**

Uncle Nathan is the King of Pumpo, and Princess Anna's fiancé. He has short **dark brown hair** and a friendly **five-day beard** that blends naturally with his **mustache**. He has warm **brown eyes** and a cheerful smile. He wears a **light brown medieval-style tunic**, held at the waist with a **black belt and gold buckle**. His trousers are a matching **dark brown**, and he wears sturdy **black boots**.

✏️ **Color Miller, Champ, and Alvin**

Miller is a happy **Golden Retriever** with short, golden-yellow fur. His ears are floppy, and he has a big, friendly smile.

Champ is a cheerful **brown dachshund** with long ears and short legs. He wears a **blue collar** with a shiny **gold dog tag**.

Alvin is a playful **orange cat** with soft fur and a fluffy tail. His eyes are bright, and he sits tall with a curious look.

✏️ **Color Tara Tara, the Mighty Golden Eagle**

Tara Tara is a majestic **golden eagle** with a strong and proud look. Her **feathers are rich brown**, while her **head and neck are bright white**. She has a sharp **golden-yellow beak** and strong **yellow talons** with dark tips. Her wide wings spread out powerfully, showing off the layers of feathers.

High above the mountains soars **Tara Tara, the Mighty Golden Eagle**. With her sharp eyes and powerful wings, she watches over the land like a true protector. Tara Tara is brave, strong, and noble—always ready to swoop in and defend her friends when they need her most.

When you color Tara Tara, remember her courage and strength. Give her bold, powerful colors to match her mighty spirit!

✏️ 🏰 Color the Breland Castle

The **Breland Castle** stands tall and proud on a hill, watching over the kingdom. Its strong stone walls keep everyone safe, and its tall red rooftops shine brightly in the sun. Behind the castle, rolling green hills and snow-topped mountains stretch as far as the eye can see.

When you color the Breland Castle, give the walls shades of **light gray stone** and make the **rooftops a bright red-orange**. The grass around the castle is a **lush green**, and the path leading up to the gates is made of **pale stone**. Add a **blue sky with fluffy white clouds** in the background, and don't forget the **snowy mountain peaks** far away.

This is the heart of the kingdom, so make it bold and magical—just like the adventures that begin here!

✏️ **Color Kalamazoo, Jordan, and William.**

The boys are happily pulling their little wooden wagons in the courtyard of **Breland Castle**. The stone courtyard is light tan, and the castle walls behind them are pale gray with climbing green ivy adding touches of color.

🖍 **Color Jordan and William.** From the castle's balcony they can see a convey of big trucks creating a giant cloud of dust billowing up through the village of Breland.

✏️ **Color Kalamazoo, Jordan and William.** They ran through the castle in search of King Bailey to warn him about the invasion of monster trucks.

✏️ **Color Kalamazoo, Jordan and William.** They ran outside where **Papa D** and his friend, **Mitcie** were playing pickleball.

✏️ **Color Papa D, Jordan and William.** Papa D loves his buddies.

✏ Color Kalamazoo beginning his search for Monster Trucks

✏️ **Color Kalamazoo** falls asleep along the way, in search of the Invading Monster Trucks.

✏️ **Color Kalamazoo's** dreams about Monster Trucks...

✏️ ...he dreams of Monster Trucks smashing houses, fences, and mailboxes...

✏️ …and **Kalamazoo** dreams of battling the **Dough Monster**…

✏️ ...and escaping the soda shop explosion.

✏️ **Color Kalamazoo** stopping bucket trucks. They weren't Monster Trucks after all.

✏️ **Color Kalamazoo Riding Tara Tara back to the castle.**

Kalamazoo is flying high on **Tara Tara's** back! Kalamazoo wears his red headband, cream shirt, brown vest, green pants, and brown boots. Tara Tara has golden-brown feathers, a white head, and a bright yellow beak and talons. Use the same colors you've used before to bring them to life as they soar together across the sky.

✏️ **Color Kalamazoo** explaining his adventures and discovery to **King Bailey** and **Queen Ashley.**

✏️ **Color King Bailey and Queen Ashley.**

✏️ **Color King Bailey** hugging **Jordan and William goodbye** after explaining to them that he is an electrical lineman when he isn't home being the King of Breland.

Activity Page

<< Maze / Word Search / Connect the Dots >>

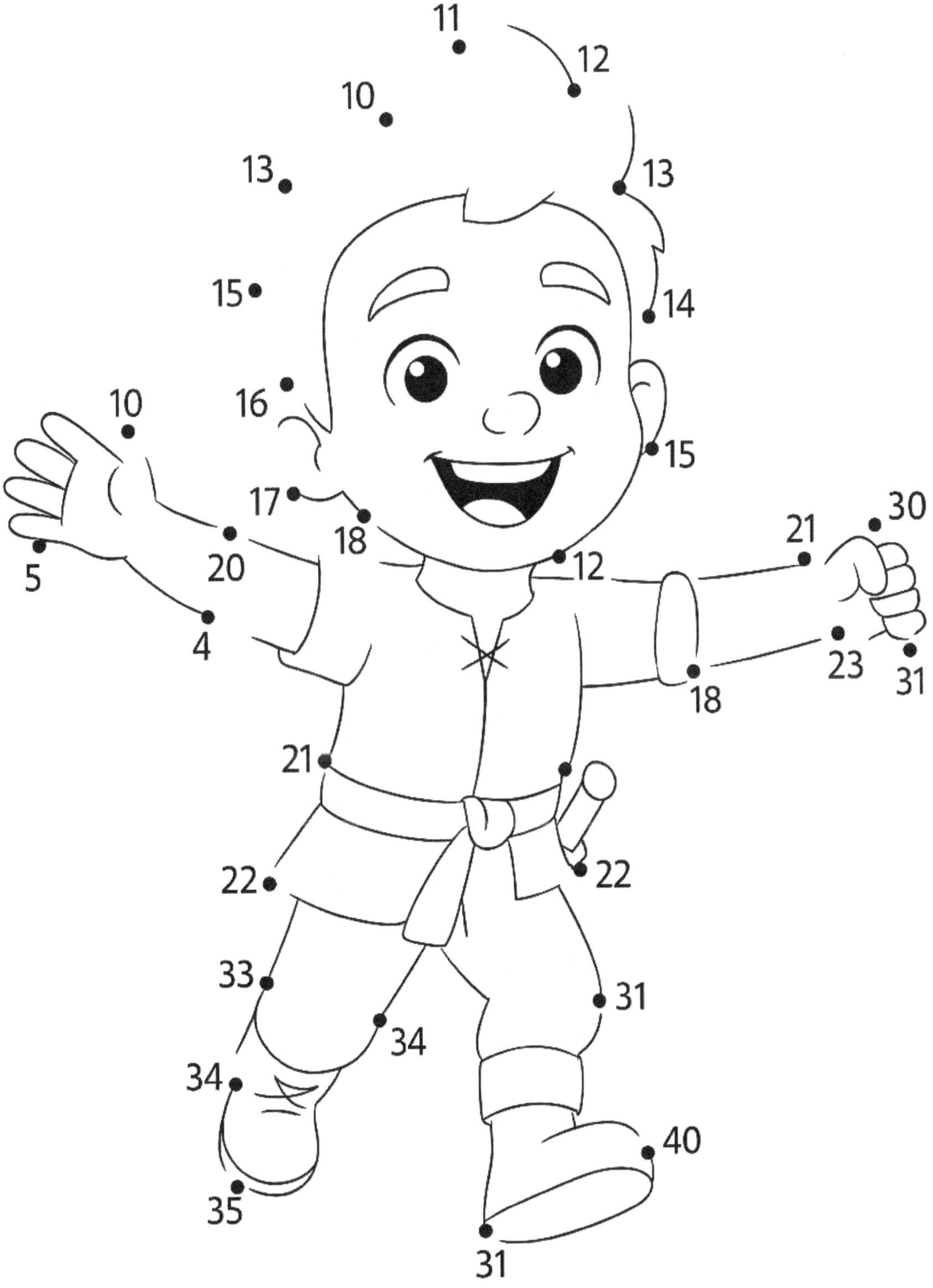

Draw Your Own Adventure!

<< Blank bordered page for doodles >>

Congratulations!

You've completed the Color Me, Kalamazoo coloring book!

Draw Your Own Adventure! (Page 1)

Draw Your Own Adventure! (Page 2)

Draw Your Own Adventure! (Page 3)

Good night,

sleep tight!

Subscribe to Kalamazoo's YouTube Channel,
@AdventuresofKalamazoo

to find

the cartoon series,

Me and You and Kalamazoo

on TV!